ALL HANDS ON DECK

Tales from the Table

SUZANNE ANISFELD

This edition first published in paperback by
Michael Terence Publishing in 2023
www.mtp.agency

ISBN 9781800945807

Images
courtesy of Suzanne Anisfeld

Illustrations
by Jacob M Wolf

Michael Terence
Publishing

This book is dedicated to my parents, Irene and Marcel,
who introduced me to card games at an early age.

Foreword

I have been involved in bridge all of my adult life: playing, working and enjoying. I have travelled the world running events, teaching classes and giving seminars. I come at the game of bridge from a professional point of view. I try to get across to people what a wonderful game it is.

Suzanne Anisfeld is a lady who has been caught with the bridge bug. I met Suzanne on my bridge events and also at the bridge table itself as well as perhaps most often, online, during the pandemic and beyond.

In this book, she tells a great variety of stories in which bridge has become interwoven in her life. With a balance of humour, intrigue and interest, she tells how bridge can colour one's life.

Read this book and you will find how a simple card game can change *your* life!

- Bernard Magee -

Having played bridge now for over thirty-five years, I thought I would put pen to paper and share some of my experiences with you, not necessarily from the bridge table and you do not need to understand the game to read this book. Although by the end of it, I hope you may consider learning this incredible game.

For ease of reference, duplicate bridge is a competitive form of the game where all the players in the room play the same hands and the scores are compared against others.

Ok, that's enough of the bridge lesson for today, let's go!

- Suzanne -

Contents

Openings

bridge

noun: **bridge**; plural noun: **bridges**

1. a structure carrying a road, path, railway, etc. across a river, road, or other obstacle.

   "a bridge across the river Thames"

   Similar:

   viaduct
   aqueduct
   overpass
   flyover
   way over

2. something intended to reconcile or connect two seemingly incompatible things.

   "a committee which was formed to create a **bridge between** rival party groups"

   Similar:

   link
   connection
   means of uniting
   bond
   tie

   a. short for land bridge.

3. the elevated, enclosed platform on a ship from which the captain and officers direct operations.

   "Talbot stepped across the two gunwales and made his way up to the bridge"

4. the upper bony part of a person's nose.

   "he pushed his spectacles further up the bridge of his nose"

   a. the central part of a pair of glasses, fitting over the bridge of the nose.

   "these sunglasses have a special nose bridge for comfort"

5. a partial denture supported by natural teeth on either side.

6. the part of a stringed instrument over which the strings are stretched.

   "ebony bridges and fingerboards"

7. a bridge passage or middle eight in music

8. the support for the tip of a billiard cue formed by the hand.

   a. a long stick with a frame at the end which is used to support a cue for a difficult shot.

9. an electric circuit with two branches across which a detector or load is connected, used to measure resistance or other property by equalizing the potential across the two ends of a detector, or to rectify an alternating voltage or current.

verb: **bridge**; 3rd person present: **bridges**; past tense: **bridged**; past participle: **bridged**; gerund or present participle: **bridging**

1. be or make a bridge over (something).

   "a covered walkway bridged the gardens"

At the fairly tender age of twenty, I had been dating my boyfriend for just over a year, and he asked if he could teach me how to play bridge. I had never even heard of the game "bridge". The only bridges I knew were the dictionary definitions above but why was this game not listed? Ian had just recently finished university where he had a regular bridge partner but wanted to introduce the game to me so I could now take over as his partner. Of course, I seemed to love the game right from the start, having always played card games with my family. I was and still am a born shuffler. I am sure I could shuffle before I started walking and talking! I could see that this game was different from all other card games that I had played and certainly a lot more challenging and exciting.

The majority of the games were played with Ian as my bridge partner and his parents as the opponents. Together, we would sit and play for many hours, teaching me new conventions and ideas and boosting my confidence at the card table. Surely enough, our bridge partnership was getting stronger as was our relationship. He also had to check that I liked bridge before proposing! So, I accepted his marriage proposal to be his partner in life and also at the card table.

Over the years, pretty much every time we played, my mother-in-law would end up throwing her cards all over the floor. You see, having your regular bridge partner as your spouse may not necessarily be a good idea! My father-in-law would say, "Marian, I cannot believe that you bid the hand that way and as for your play…" So, she would end up getting very angry. And Ian or I would say, "Dad, after twenty-five years of playing together, we can't understand that you haven't realized that she isn't as good as you!" And this same conversation would happen almost every time we played. But such was her love for the game that she would always come back to the table and resume where we left off. Fortunately, the cards were not thrown on the floor twice in one evening!

Apart from playing with us, my in-laws used to have a regular social game with their close friends, Frank and Sandra. One snowy Sunday evening, they went round for a light supper followed by a few hands, but not as many as they would have wished to play. You see, at about half past nine, whilst he was dummy, Frank went upstairs and a couple of minutes later came down in his pyjamas. "I'm tired and am going to sleep now!" My in-laws couldn't believe what they were seeing but didn't want to outstay their welcome so took their coats and left. Quite upset about it, they got back into their car which unfortunately wouldn't start. They tried absolutely everything but had no luck. This was before the days of mobile phones, so they had no choice but to hesitantly ring their friends' doorbell. "Our car has broken down; please can we use your phone to call the AA?" Of course, they let them call but then sent my in-laws back to their car in the freezing cold to wait for help. And that, I believe, was the end of a beautiful friendship.

Ian and I had entered a charity league where we played matches in people's homes. We were sent a list of four or five pairs that were local to us and went along to Michelle and Adam for our first match. We got on very well with them and Michelle and Ian were in the same line of business so had a lot of common ground. I cannot remember very much about the game but on one particular hand, Ian was dealt all black cards, which is only spades and clubs, also known as "two-suited". Ian was so excited, started jumping for joy and had to phone his father who had been playing bridge for over forty years and had never been two-suited in his life!

Having had a failed fertility treatment, we needed to get away and my mum told me that one of her friends was organizing a week's bridge holiday overseas; perhaps we would like to join? To lift our spirits, we decided to go and enjoy a week of sunshine and some bridge. Despite feeling rather low, we had a lovely time and what made it even better was that we won the overall competition.

A few months later, we went back to Nottingham for our second treatment. Driving back home to London, we had a duplicate tournament in the evening, which turned out to be the first of many. We remained in the North/South position all evening as I was being extra vigilant and didn't want to be bobbing up and down the whole time. The treatment was successful, and I was the happiest girl in the world.

In the summer of 1996, my parents-in-law decided to leave London and spend their retirement years in Bournemouth. You can imagine how distraught we were. Firstly, as I was pregnant with their first grandchild, I thought, how inconvenient that they seemed to be getting out of their grandparental duties; babysitting wouldn't be so easy if we wanted to go out for the evening. I wouldn't expect them to drive to London just for our convenience. More importantly, we would not be continuing with our regular bridge game which I was really enjoying. Who would we end up playing bridge with? Most of the players we knew did not fit into our age category!

♣ ♦ ♠ ♥

Challenging

I used to enjoy taking part in quizzes and I decided to apply to be on the television program "Fifteen to One." I have no idea why I selected this as my general knowledge was not up to scratch. However, I was accepted onto the program, and it was a very nerve-wracking experience. In the first round, fifteen people were asked two questions and if they got both wrong, they were out of the game.

My first question was, "What are the rising currents of warm air called that are used by glider pilots to gain height?"

I had absolutely no idea and couldn't even hazard a guess. The answer was "Thermals". Who knew that? Not me!

My second question: "What is the date that is written on the tablet held by the Statue of Liberty?"

Phew, I knew this one, 4th July 1776.

Now I was through to the second round. The host, William G Stewart, began by asking a question to the first person who was still in. If they answered correctly, they could then start to nominate other players. Anyhow, we were all standing in a semi-circle and I was positioned at number 9, almost in the centre of the curve. Questions were flying all over me and no-one seemed to be picking on me. We were down to four people and I was getting very excited as the final three people standing would go through to the last round. Finally, someone nominated me.

Question: Suzanne, playing cards, how many face cards are there in a standard pack of cards?

With less than three seconds to answer, "Sixteen," I said confidently which was followed by an incorrect "beep". Of course, I was counting the Aces as well. The answer was twelve. I cannot believe that I was out on a question about cards. They could have asked me a question on Astrophysics, History,

Ancient Greek or basically anything. But playing cards? How could I go wrong?

A few months later, whilst lying in my bed, no not my bed at home but the hospital bed about to pop, both my parents and my in-laws were waiting around eagerly expecting their grandchild. I was induced but baby did not want to come out and nothing was happening. You'll never guess what my in-laws asked. Did we fancy a game of bridge? And of course, when you are a keen bridge player, you always have a pack of cards in your handbag. So, believe it or not, we played, and it was a great way of passing the time. I cannot remember if the three others were standing or sitting but I was definitely lying down. The only thing that I do remember, my mother-in-law was rather slow at playing her cards out and I couldn't resist saying, "Come on Mum, I haven't got all day!"

Playing bridge in the maternity ward with the in-laws

Many people that I know started learning bridge at school or university, then would take a break for many years whilst bringing up their family and would resume much later in life. Not me! The children had to fit in wherever bridge took me. I used to play a regular Friday afternoon game with the girls when Natalie was only a few months old and fortunately, as I wasn't breastfeeding, whoever was dummy used to take turns to feed her.

Having my in-laws in Bournemouth was a wonderful thing. Firstly, we now had a social game set up on a weekly basis with a couple of our friends and would also go around to my brother and sister-in-law's house to help teach her, so our previous regular bridge game with the in-laws now became a regular holiday bridge session. We spent many holidays there with the children. Going on lovely walks, having fun at the seaside and many an adventurous day out, after an early supper all together, the two children would be flat out and we would put them to bed at around 7 o'clock. The four of us would then play until 2 in the morning. Of course, twenty minutes went on sorting out the cards that my mother-in-law had previously thrown on the floor.

By the time the children were 9 and 7, unfortunately, the marriage was not working so we decided to go our separate ways. Despite our differences, I do however have Ian to thank for a couple of things. Number 1, The Children, Number 2, Bridge. Although not necessarily in that order!

♣ ♦ ♠ ♥

Singleton

Apart from getting used to the single life again and raising two young children on my own, I knew that I didn't want to give up playing bridge. My ex-husband was the only person I had ever partnered and I was very nervous and apprehensive about finding someone else. But the love of the game helped me to find new partnerships and I didn't settle for just one regular partner but a few. I do believe that improved my bridge play as I had to learn to adapt to their systems.

Talking of partnerships, I soon realized that I wanted some romance in my life, preferably with someone who had mutual interests in travel, theatre and hopefully bridge. But where does a woman in her late thirties meet eligible gentlemen? All my friends were married and didn't have any suitable single gentlemen friends. So of course, it had to be online dating. This was an eye-opening experience for me, and I had quite a lot of fun with it, to be honest.

I got chatting to a man I had met at a quiz who seemed to be quite nice. And he was single. So, he asked me out on a date. He had been using the same Internet dating site as me, but we hadn't come across each other whilst scanning the site. Talking to him on the phone one afternoon, I told him to log onto the website at the same time as me as they had quiz questions where you could challenge a friend. So, we both logged on.

His first question was, "How many degrees are there in a right angle?"

While I was hanging onto the end of the phone, I saw his answer come up on the screen, "2".

"What?" I said, "everyone knows there are 90 degrees in a right angle."

His response was, "Well, Maths isn't my strong point."

Ok, I thought, let's see the next question. "Who sang Goldfinger?"

"Aretha Franklin," he replied.

Oh dear, I thought to myself, I am pretty sure it was Shirley Bassey.

And his final question, "Where is Mount Olympus?" Yes, wait for it, his answer, "America."

"Have you not heard of the Olympic Games?" I asked. "The answer is Greece!"

To which came the response, "Well, geography isn't my strong point."

After a long deliberation of about three seconds, he was dumped!

I do remember going to friends for dinner a few weeks later and telling them the three-question story and they found the whole thing rather amusing. The men suggested that they wouldn't want to go on a date with me as they would have to take their atlas and dictionary with them.

I agreed to meet a gentleman that I had met on the dating site for supper at a local restaurant. He was very interesting to talk to but there was no attraction there. However, he did play bridge. Nothing came of our meeting but after a couple of weeks, I heard about a bridge competition which I wanted to enter but I didn't have a partner. So, I contacted him, and he agreed to partner me. I think he was quite a good player, but I cannot remember how well or badly we did in the competition.

At the end of the evening, he said to me, "I thought you weren't interested?" Just because I contacted him for a game of bridge, does that really mean anything else?

♣ ♦ ♠ ♥

Fun and Games

Online dating and spending lots of time on the computer led me to find out that you can actually play bridge online. How incredible is that? You can play bridge at any time of the day and you don't need to get dressed up; you can even play bridge whilst you're in bed! I am not a big reader so I don't have a book by my bed, but I do have my laptop. I spent many hours playing bridge on BCL (Bridge Club Live), became "friends" with many people and formed quite a few new online partnerships. I used to play online when I went to bed and on many occasions, fell asleep at the table. In fact, I think I was even banned once or twice from using the site.

One of the players on the site was a gentleman from Kenya. We got chatting whilst waiting for other players to join our table. He could see from my profile that I was living in NW London, but he didn't know where, so he asked me. I didn't think a man from Kenya would have heard of Stanmore so I mentioned Edgware which would have had slightly more chance. "How funny, my daughter lives in Canons Park," which is the next town to Edgware, and she had an optician shop next to the station. It turned out that the lady used to be my optician. What a small world!

By now, I was really addicted to Bridge Club Live; playing in the morning as I woke and late at night when I went to bed. Sometimes, I even played in the office. One day, I was left alone in the office as my boss and colleagues had gone out. I had finished my work for the day, but I still had a couple of hours left at the office. So, what did I do? I logged onto BCL and was enjoying a great game for about half an hour. I was about to play a hand in "seven no trumps" which means that you must make all thirteen tricks and you get a great bonus score for bidding and making it. I would say that bidding "seven no trumps" only comes up maybe once every three or four months and is probably equivalent to a royal flush in poker.

The dummy's cards came down on the table and I looked at the cards and my cards and planned my play. I was so excited as I could see that I was going to make my contract and get a great score. Just as I was about to play my first card, I could hear footsteps coming towards me. OMG, my boss had just walked back into the office and he had a full view of my computer screen. I didn't think he would be too impressed with my playing bridge and not working. So, what could I do? I pressed the X button at the top of the screen and never got to complete the hand. You can imagine how annoyed I was.

When I got home, I sent a message to all the other players at the table and told them that my internet connection had gone and what great timing was that!

Having spent many holidays away with my children, we had wonderful times together although I did miss playing bridge. I tried to teach them as they loved card games, but they suggested they were far too young to learn and would contemplate it in fifty years' time! Hanging around at airports waiting to board my flights, I would log on to my iPad on BCL and start playing. My kids literally had to drag me off my seat to board the plane as quite often, we would nearly miss our flight!

Just after the summer holidays, my friend Lesley agreed to partner me in a charity league competition where the first round ran from September through to December; and the second round from January to April. Fortunately, we got through to the finals which was held at the Selfridge Hotel on Baker Street in May. This was the first time that both of us had played together in a duplicate event, and we were very excited to be there.

A delicious buffet was served to sixty-four players before the bridge commenced. Lesley and I were sitting in the East/West position so had no idea of how we were doing during the evening because we were not in control of the Bridgemate scorer. At the end of the game, the tournament director handed out printed results sheets to all sixteen tables. We looked down the long list of names which were ranked in order and to our surprise, we could not see our names on the list which we thought was rather strange. So, we called over the director.

"Ladies, please turn the page over," and there we were, right at the bottom of the list!

Back to dating; whenever I started speaking to any potential suitors, I would ask those three questions, you know the right angle, Shirley Bassey and Olympic, and if they didn't get all three correct, they wouldn't get a look in.

I did, however, meet someone online who confidently gave the correct answers, and he would soon become my second husband. Unfortunately, he didn't play bridge and the marriage only lasted a couple of years. I could write another book about everything I went through, but I really don't want to waste any time or effort on that complete waste of space, so let's move on.

Several months later, one Sunday afternoon, I decided to re-register on the online dating site to see if there was anyone that took my fancy. There was a face that I recognized from the local village Facebook group; someone who organized local Sunday walks. Strangely enough, I nearly went on one of his walks the previous year when I was married.

Anyway, without reading his profile, I decided to send a very short message,

"Hello, just want to say that I recognize you from the Facebook Village Group." Then I returned to BCL.

After playing for half an hour or so, a noise I didn't recognize came from my computer. On further investigation, I realized it was a message notification from the dating site.

"Hi, I'm Irving and pleased to receive your message. How funny that you recognize me from Facebook. I assume you are local?"

So, I was reading his message whilst trying to concentrate on my cards and it was now my turn to play out one of the hands.

My message to Irving was, "You will have to excuse me, but I am a very sad person who is addicted to a card game called bridge and right now, I am actually playing a hand online so I cannot chat."

"I play bridge," he replied.

Well, all I can say now is, the rest is history. Irving is my boyfriend and having been together now for ten years, we share so many passions, musical theatre, eating out, walking, quizzes, badminton to name but a few and of course, bridge. I should also add that he correctly answered those 3 questions.

Soon after meeting Irving, I received a text message from my sister-in-law, Rene, asking if I would enter a bridge tournament with her. Well, I got the shock of my life as Rene had been learning the game for many years and had weekly sessions with a group of friends on a Tuesday morning. Quite often, I had asked her to come and play in some of my events, but if it was not a Tuesday, she wouldn't play. Tuesday was the only day of the week that was devoted to bridge. But this tournament she had asked me to play in was taking place on a Monday.

I called her and asked for some clarification. You see Rene had never played any duplicate bridge before. Her friends had asked her in the past to join events which she would always decline. I am not sure why this competition was any different but finally, she told her friends that she would enter; but only if she could partner me.

I was sorry to disappoint her but I was moving house four days after the event and thought that I would be too busy packing boxes. She made me feel very guilty as this would be her very first event and she would be honoured to partner me. How could I refuse? We were so happy to win the competition and to this date, I believe this is the only time she has played duplicate bridge. Her silver plate is proudly displayed in her home with very fond memories of her very first and very last win!

♣ ♦ ♠ ♥

Healing Hands

Approximately eight years ago, Irving and I took over the running of the Cancer Research UK Bridge Tournament, set up by Judy and Ray Cecil in honour of their daughter Jane who died from leukaemia at the age of eighteen. The competition started approximately forty-five years ago. In those days, there were roughly eight hundred applicants, and this was before the age of emails. All application forms were sent out in the post with stamps. Judy and Ray had to handwrite every single envelope. For me, it is easy. Of course, you are talking to Miss Spreadsheet here and there is absolutely no way I would have organized this event without a computer.

During a finals event for the CRUK competition, held at a central London hotel, we came across an elderly lady who was a very good player. She was also a chain smoker and literally between every couple of hands that were played, she would go outside to light up. When playing against her, Irving told her that it was not good for her health and didn't think it was appropriate for her to be smoking, especially at a Cancer charity event.

To which her response was, "I am ninety-three years old and have been smoking all my life, I think it agrees with me!"

Apart from partnering in the CRUK bridge league, Irving and I would play a fair amount of social bridge and frequent some of the local bridge clubs. On one occasion, we were seated with a couple of infamous players whose reputation at the club was of being rather obnoxious. In bridge, the final contract is decided once there is a bid followed by three sequential passes. It was quite an auction, but the ending to it was a "three no trumps" bid by the opponent sitting at North position, then a pass from me followed by a pass by Steve at South. Before Irving had a chance to make a bid, Steve wished his partner good luck in playing the contract. Irving told him that was a little presumptuous as you couldn't just assume that he, Irving was going to pass.

Steve got up from his seat and proclaimed, "This is my life."

And he wanted to take Irving outside to punch him. Some people just take this game far too seriously!

Once, on playing at the Acol bridge club, Irving and I were sitting in the East/West position which means after each round of a couple of hands that lasts approximately fifteen minutes, you would move on to the next table in a clockwise direction whilst the hands moved in an anti-clockwise direction. We find that we like playing E/W as walking from one table to another is about the only exercise we do during the day. You see, the hazards of bridge are sitting at the table for far too long and we really like to stretch our legs. The person sitting in the north position takes control of the "Bridgemate" which is the bridge scorer. Anyhow, as Irving and I moved on to the next table, I didn't recognize the people that we were about to play. The Bridgemate showed our names so our new opponents would know who was joining their table.

On taking our seats, North who was Danny, announced, "Hi Suzanne, it's lovely to meet you. Did you know that we are cousins, and you are on my family tree?"

Well, I had never even heard of Danny and had to ask my parents who he was to which my father explained that he was some distant blood relative. It also turned out that Danny was a bridge author and a top player. I, therefore, believe that our mutual love of the game must be in the genes.

Five years ago, Irving and I were playing in another charity bridge league and came across two very nice gentlemen for a game at my house. It was a great game, and we were getting all the cards. I felt somewhat embarrassed as I didn't feel that I was being very hospitable as at every hand we were picking up incredible cards. To add insult to injury, on the penultimate hand, my partner was dealt twenty-nine points to which we landed up in a "six no trump" contract and made twelve tricks with a somewhat rather fortunate lead. A couple of months later, my children surprised me with a very nice 50th birthday tea at which that twenty-nine-point bridge hand ended up on my birthday cake.

We went around to our friends for a social bridge game and were talking about a lady who used to run one of the local bridge clubs. Unfortunately, she had become quite unwell and was finding it too difficult to run the club.

Just as I was playing out my cards, I muttered under my breath, "Perhaps we should run the club?"

And Sylvia looked at me and said, "Yes."

To which I replied, "What? I'm only joking!"

Well, that was the start of our business bridge partnership, and the "Heath Club" was born.

♣ ♦ ♠ ♥

In The Club

Running a club is not as easy as you would think. Firstly, because we did not have a card sorting machine, we had to arrange for someone to do this for us and we would pick up five briefcases of cards from him on a monthly basis. We also had to learn how to direct a club for which we attended the English Bridge Union for a director's course. And you had to be fairly capable of using the computer to show the weekly tournament results and send out regular emails about our sessions. Unfortunately, my degree in Maths, Computing and Statistics wasn't much of an aid as back in the day, my computer training was learning the languages of BASIC and PASCAL. Really not much help!

In addition to the bridge side of things, we would have to set up the tables and chairs and put out all the bridge equipment. It isn't that simple; there are the tables and chairs, the table covers, the bidding boxes, the bridge score sheets, the pens and the bridge travellers and knowing how many tables to set each week was also a bit of a challenge. In addition, we had to provide refreshments. We used to make freshly-baked cakes and biscuits each week and also serve coffee, tea and cold drinks. Unfortunately, I am not a very keen chef and even though my eldest sister has an incredible talent for baking, these skills did not rub off on her baby sister.

As well as directing in a club, I also started teaching bridge to beginners. One lady contacted me and told me that unfortunately, she was already learning with a group of three other bridge friends but had to drop out due to ill health. So having recovered, she wanted some lessons to catch up on a few of the basic techniques. I went around to her house; she was about the same age as me and had recently remarried. Her husband was not a bridge player and wasn't interested in learning the game, but this was something she wanted to do with her girlfriends.

Having first talked about some of the bidding techniques, I got out my pack of cards and dealt the pack into four piles. She picked up her hand and sorted the cards into suits. I then asked her to count how many points she had. "Fourteen," she replied, and I told her to add up again. The next attempt was seventeen; the third attempt was twelve and finally, she then told me to count the points. I will now explain that in bridge, all the playing cards numbered 2 to 10 have no point value, but the Ace is worth 4 points, the King is worth 3, the Queen 2 and finally the Jack is 1. So, if you add up all the points in the pack, it comes to 10 points for each suit and as there are 4 suits, this will equate to a total of forty points. This comes completely naturally to me and is like shelling peas. I really cannot understand how people struggle in working out how many points they hold.

Anyway, as far as not adding up her points properly, she also had trouble with some of the basic conventions. She then told me that she was good at languages; clearly, she hadn't grasped the language of bridge. I suggested perhaps she would be better off doing something else, maybe learning a new language or starting art classes. I assumed that she obviously enjoyed learning bridge.

"No," she retorted, "I hate it!"

Why on earth would someone wish to do something they hated? It is not compulsory, and bridge is not for everyone. I just don't get it.

♣ ♦ ♠ ♥

Travellers

Having spent an evening at Michelle and Adam's, they told us that they had recently come back from Dublin. One of Michelle's old school friends, who was recently retired, had a passion for travel and a love for Guinness. He had a crazy idea that he was going to visit every European capital city and drink a pint at a pub. Whilst drinking, he would ask the bartender to pick out of a hat the next destination. This wasn't a continuous challenge, but it did take about five years to complete. He wrote a blog about all his experiences and set up a website with all the information to be seen. He also advised friends of his next destination in case anyone wanted to meet up with him on his travels. His final destination was Dublin, home of the Guinness factory and about fifty of his friends and family joined him as he completed his challenge.

Well, I thought this story was fantastic and decided that I wanted to do something like that. The problem was, I didn't like Guinness! So how could I fit this challenge somewhere into my life? I know – it must be a bridge challenge. Michelle and Adam who also were keen bridge players, together with Irving and me had come up with the idea of travelling to all the English counties and playing one game of bridge in a local club. So, one weekend in October 2019, we set off to Devon and Cornwall and had a couple of games. We enjoyed a lovely weekend also taking in the sights of Stonehenge and The Eden Project. And enroute home, we stopped off in Bristol where Michelle's brother lived who made us a lovely dinner. I would personally like to thank Adam for all the driving; don't worry, next time we will drive!

♣ ♦ ♠ ♥

Top Tricks

Early the next month, I read online about a charity bridge event to take place in the City of London in February 2020 where you had the opportunity of partnering a bridge professional. The list of professionals was shown on the site, and you then had to make a bid of money for a player of your choice. Although a very keen player, I was unaware of who the professionals were, but I scanned the list and had heard of a couple of them. Jeremy Dhondy who had recently retired as Chairman of the English Bridge Union was on the list and I thought he must know how to play bridge so I will bid for him. Between November and February, if someone made a bid for a higher price, I would receive an email to notify me and ask if I wanted to up my stakes.

Fortunately for me, no other bids were made, and I won Jeremy for the evening! The event was held at the Stationers Hall, and we had to get dressed up for the evening. A special guest at the event was Victoria Coren Mitchell, the host of "Only Connect", an international poker player and a dab hand at the bridge table. A very nice buffet dinner was presented before the bridge play where I had the chance to speak to Jeremy and discuss what bridge systems we were going to use later in the evening.

Well, it was a very friendly atmosphere and as we moved from table to table, people would say "Hello, Jeremy, how are you? And who is your partner for tonight?" Of course, everyone knew Jeremy, having been the Chairman of the EBU but I didn't know anyone, apart from one or two familiar faces who I had previously met at a couple of the bridge clubs.

On the evening, the bridge was very average. Nothing exciting happened at the table i.e., no grand slams, no doubling of contracts and I felt that there was no particular advantage of partnering Jeremy. I think I could have done just as well with my regular partner. In the penultimate round, we came across two ladies who clearly didn't know Jeremy. They were, however, very friendly, and the play commenced.

Victoria Coren Mitchell and me.

On the Bridgemate scoring machine which I have previously told you about, you enter the score of each hand, and it comes up with a percentage of how you have done in that particular hand. The first hand against these ladies, I played in a "six diamond" contract and made my twelve tricks which scored us over 90%. Jeremy looked at me and congratulated me on my bid and play and suggested that he wouldn't have ended up in a slam. On the next hand, the ladies ended up in a "two heart" contract which gave us a 100% as everyone else in the room had bid and made "four hearts". I was so delighted to receive these two great scores. One of the ladies looked at the two of us and asked, "Which one of you is the pro?" Well, you can imagine how happy I was to receive this wonderful compliment and it was certainly worth paying a lot of money for that!

Me and Jeremy Dhondy.

♣ ♦ ♠ ♥

Passed Out

Over the course of a few months, I was busy organizing a charity bridge event which I was getting very excited about. This event is known as Café Bridge, and it is playing duplicate bridge with a twist. Rather like a pub crawl, you start off playing a few hands in a café or restaurant and after your first set of boards, you move on to the next restaurant and play some more hands et cetera et cetera. You have approximately six rounds of bridge and wherever you are playing at the third round, you end up eating lunch there.

Well, I had almost two hundred people signed up for this unusual event and I was getting very busy, organizing the restaurants, and sorting out raffle prizes. The date of the event was 24 March 2020 and had been advertised for about six months. This date may be familiar to you and a few weeks before, the numbers started dropping like flies. 23 March, PM Boris Johnson made a statement that affected the whole country; we would be going into lockdown commencing the next day, my bridge event! You can imagine how disappointed I was but obviously, I had no alternative but to cancel and would hopefully be able to organize another one in the not-too-distant future.

One of the emails that I received in relation to this was very much appreciated:

> Dear Suzanne,
>
> I just wanted to thank you for ensuring that we all stay as safe as possible, at the same time raising so much for such a worthy cause.
>
> Thinking about how easy it would have been for at least one of us to have gone down with the rampaging virus by going ahead with the Heath Club or the Café Bridge Day, you should be very proud of yourself for your wise

decisions notwithstanding the cost to yourself and Sylvia when you have made such a good job of reviving the Heath Club through your hard work. I am relieved for you that you can hold your head up high knowing that you have probably saved at least one life given the vulnerability of most of the Heath Club members and I don't doubt reducing the opportunity of the virus spreading itself further to the contacts and families of the bridge club members and the would-be Café Bridge Day participants.

I have always admired you for your charitable work and seemingly indefatigable energy in organising so many bridge competitions for charity. You are now top of my list of role models in this difficult time for us all.

I hope you and yours stay safe and well and we can look forward to our Café Bridge Day again and returning to a resurrected Heath Club in the not-too-distant future.

Kindest regards.

♣ ♦ ♠ ♥

Vulnerable

Lockdown, what a very strange time this was for me, my family, my friends, the whole country and yes, the whole world. What was I going to do? What were we all going to do? More importantly, what were we allowed to do? Fortunately, the previous month I had just completed the 'Couch to 5K' programme which basically got me running for a constant thirty-minute period from not being able to run five yards. I don't think I achieved the 5K target, but it was about 3.5K and I was feeling very proud of myself. The timing couldn't have been any better as we were allowed to do our daily exercises and running was a great way of getting out of the house.

Obviously, all my face-to-face games were not allowed but thank goodness for the online site. I had been introduced to a new website, Bridge Base Online, otherwise known as BBO and so many of my friends seemed to have signed up to it. Running, online bridge and getting used to working from home became my whole new routine. Shopping for groceries for my parents, dropping it all off to them and seeing them from a distance was very difficult and upsetting. But we had no choice and soon got used to our new way of life.

I started teaching bridge online via Zoom. I had a couple of groups set up where we would open up both the BBO page and the Zoom page at the same time. They didn't need to see me but hear me, so I could give advice about their bids and play. On one occasion, I had a group of four ladies and I set up a teaching table, so I was able to see everyone's cards. The first thing that I did was to get all the ladies to count their points. Once they had added them up, I asked them to announce their point count. They promptly announced in clockwise order: Fifteen; eleven; five and then there was a hesitation while we waited for the fourth lady to count. I reminded her about the card values, and she continued to count. Another long pause while we were waiting for her to announce 'nine'.

"Oh, I have it, 120!"

I couldn't contain my laughter, and neither could the other ladies and even Miss 120 joined in on all the fun.

Another of the ladies was struggling to tell the difference between the Nine of Diamonds and the Nine of Clubs. Surely, every woman knows what a diamond looks like!

You really need a lot of patience to teach this game which I believe I must have.

During the lockdown period, I was sent a poem from one of my bridge friends with the following message:

I'm giving up bridge - tonight's my last night
It's amen to Stayman, I give up the fight.
The insults and muddles are giving me troubles
And I can't sleep at night for thinking of doubles.

My cards are all rotten and I have forgotten
Who's played and what's trumps and what's gone on my right!
So, for now, it's all over - I'm off to the back wood
I'm bidding goodbye to Gerber and Blackwood.

I can't stand the hassle, I can't stand the pain
I'm getting those bad cards again and again.
So, I'm giving up bridge - tonight's a bad night
Declarer is horrid and nothing's gone right.

My partner's a dope and I'm losing all hope
And when he says "double", I know we're in trouble
My points are not high and I'm wondering why
He kept on bidding right up to the sky.

We're in seven spades and all my hope fades
When surprise, surprise, the high bidding pays.
We're winning all tricks; the defenders feel sick
And I have to admit my partner's a brick.

But I'm giving up bridge - tonight's my last night
Farewell to conventions - I give up the fight.
So, I leave with few words but some that are true
Bridge is a game - not for me but for you.

So be kind to your partners and don't mind their cheek
For it's only a game - Oh! Yes. I'll see you next week!

How funny is that? So of course, I was busy texting all my bridge friends. A response from one of them which made me giggle was, "Lol! Please don't give up, bridge needs you."

I received a phone call from a friend asking if I would enter a bridge tournament being run by her tennis club in a couple of weeks. They needed one more person as someone had just dropped out and Sue knew that I would never say no to a game of bridge. The tennis club used to have a weekly bridge game before Covid but was now running sessions online. Sue said she would give my telephone number to Anthony who was organising the sessions and he would contact me to confirm the details.

Literally, as soon as I put the phone down from Sue, I remembered that my hairdresser was coming at the same time the tournament was due to start. There was absolutely no way I could cancel the hairdresser because my hair was a complete mess; it had been months since having it cut. About 5 minutes after I spoke to Sue, Anthony phoned me and told me he was so pleased that I would be joining the session. I was sorry to disappoint him but obviously, having my hair done was much more important than a game of bridge!

I told him that I wouldn't play but if he couldn't find someone else, then perhaps I would still play at the same time as having my hair done. And this was the start of my bridge multi-tasking days. Ironing, dusting, vacuuming, all whilst playing bridge. Now that is something you definitely couldn't do at a club! And I cooked some of my best meals whilst playing online. Naturally, this is the true definition of kitchen bridge!

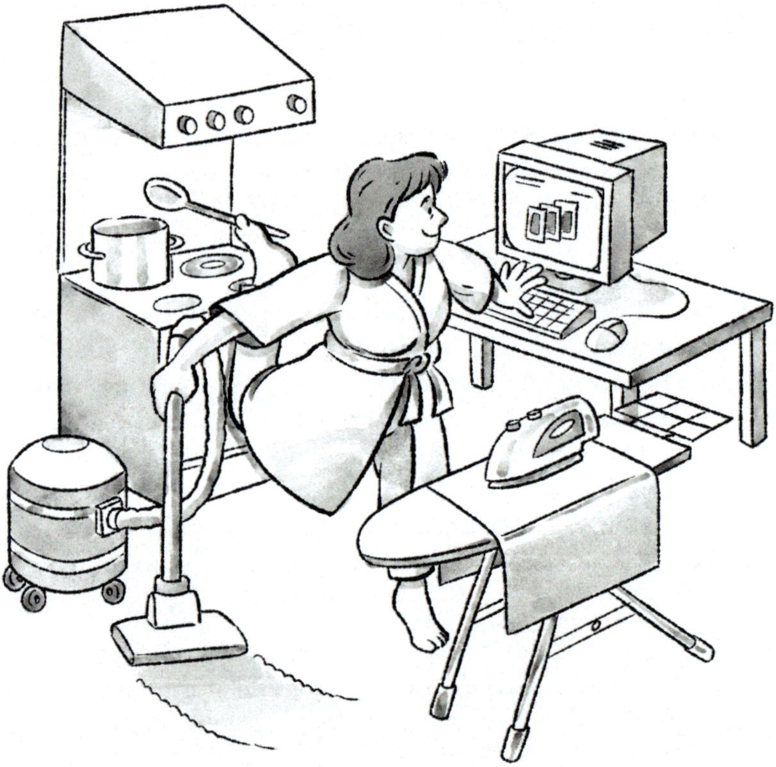

A quiet afternoon playing kitchen bridge.

♣ ♦ ♠ ♥

Call The Director

Another friend of mine told me about a twice-weekly bridge seminar taking place live on YouTube by a bridge teacher called Bernard Magee. So, what did I have to lose? At 11 a.m. on a Monday, I logged onto YouTube and was fascinated by the fact that there was a chat box where you could make comments. I was not very familiar with YouTube and its functions. Anyway, the seminars were great and Bernard had a very nice way of explaining things and putting us all at ease. He would always respond to people's questions when asked about a particular topic. I found myself typing away and probably driving him mad with my constant flow of questions.

Bernard had a PowerPoint presentation where he would type up notes on a given topic and show some sample hands that were relevant to the topic. One of the things he talked about quite a lot was "Acelessness" which basically means a hand of cards with no aces in it. Whenever he showed Aceless hands, someone would point it out and he would give that person a special mention for noticing it. On Fridays, he also played in a Teams bridge match online which consisted of 8 players, 4 in each team. He would log onto YouTube and do a live commentary which was used as part of his teaching process.

A few seminars later, one of those Aceless hands appeared on the screen and I very quickly typed "ACELESSNESS" into the chat box.

"Well done, Suzanne for saying Acelessness first," he said, "and she has won a prize. The next time I play against her, I will give her a spare Ace."

What on earth does that mean? I thought. So, I had a plan.

Pre-lockdown, I went to the famous Acol Bridge Club where I was attracted to a flyer on the noticeboard which was bordered with clubs, diamonds, hearts, and spades. This is what it said:

> The Chinese are supposed to have invented playing cards in 1000 AD.
>
> Here are some interesting facts and observations about playing cards:
>
> Did you know that the traditional deck of playing cards is a strikingly coherent form of a calendar?
>
> There are 52 weeks in the year and there are 52 playing cards in a deck.
>
> There are 13 weeks in each season and there are 13 cards in each suit.
>
> There are 4 seasons in a year and there are 4 suits in the deck.
>
> Those with faces, namely Jack, Queen and King in each suit.
>
> The red cards represent day while the black cards represent night.
>
> If you let Jacks count 11, Queens count 12, and Kings count 13, then adding up the sums of 1 (ace), 2, 3 … 13 totals 91. Multiply this by 4 for the four suits and you get 91 x 4 = 364. Add 1 that is the Joker and you will arrive at the number 365 being the days in a year.
>
> Is that a mere coincidence or a product of greater intelligence?
>
> Of interest also is the sum of the letters in all the names of the cards, adding up the letters of one, two, three, four, five, six, seven, eight, nine, ten, Jack, Queen and King give you the whole pack – 52.

So, I decided to send Bernard an email.

> Hi Bernard,
>
> Many thanks for your bridge seminars which are most helpful.
>
> I wanted to share with you a ditty (which is attached) and is quite interesting and rather fitting for me as I am going to be 52 in July. Perhaps you could share this with your viewers?
>
> Also, I was the person who mentioned "Acelessness" first today and you said you would give me a spare Ace next time I played against you! I was just thinking, would it be possible to play in your team on my birthday or against you? It would be a fab birthday present!!!
>
> Thanks, and I look forward to hearing from you.
>
> Kind regards…

Besides my love of bridge, I have a huge passion for musical theatre. I consider myself blessed to live in London where I am so lucky to be able to frequent the West End shows, cabarets and concerts on a fairly regular basis. Lockdown was a killer for those talented actors and musicians, not to mention the producers, directors, stage production teams and the list goes on. During lockdown, it was possible to sign up to live streaming of some solo artists and you could watch and listen to them from the comfort of your very own living room. But for me, there is nothing quite like live music which really plays an important part in my life.

I heard about a couple of operatic brothers who had set up their own business singing on people's doorsteps. What a wonderful idea, I thought and also to bring live music directly to you. As it was my friend Amelia's birthday, I arranged for Amanda, Alison, Gabriella, Ilana, Irving, Mark, Russell and myself to gather around in her front drive, socially distanced of course, to hear the

Doorstep Brothers sing: "Edelweiss", "It had to be you", "O Solo Mio" and "Bring Him Home". The sun was shining, and it was lovely to be with my friends again.

I returned home to an email from Bernard:

> Hi Suzanne,
>
> I think that is a reasonable request - why not!
>
> What is your username?
>
> Congratulations on winning the first quiz!
>
> Kind regards
>
> Bernard

What a great day I had. You can imagine how excited I was that I was going to be playing in the Teams match. I was telling the world, even the non-bridge players and all my friends and family were very happy for me. A few days after receiving his email, I logged on to the Monday Bernard seminar. He obviously saw my "hello everyone" in the chat box and then promptly made a comment.

"Do you remember last week I mentioned Suzanne had won a prize for being the first person to mention Acelessness? Well, she has convinced me to partner her on her birthday in the weekly Teams match."

Partner? Did he say partner? I can't believe it; I am going to be partnering Mr Magee on my birthday. What a wonderful present!

♣ ♦ ♠ ♥

King of Trumps

My son Daniel graduated from university a couple of months earlier with a degree in music. Unfortunately, it was not a good time for the music industry as everyone was stuck at home. So, no job. However, he started creating birthday and anniversary videos using his musical talent and editing skills which did provide him with a little income. On the morning of my birthday, he presented me with a wonderful half-hour video. To my surprise, he had contacted many of our family and my friends and given them one line of the song by Carole King, "You've Got a Friend" and merged them all together, with him on keyboard playing the backing.

Some of my friends are tone-deaf and Daniel found this a bit of a challenge as he had to keep changing key to make the song sound half-decent. At the end of the song, there were messages from friends who chose not to sing and left me a birthday message instead. The final message was from Bernard wishing me good luck for the evening. Even though I didn't "see" anyone on my birthday, this was one of the best birthdays ever!

The following week my friend Val and I signed up for a charity online bridge event. Anthony from the tennis club happened to be watching us online as he had "friended" me on BBO since I was due to play in his club's session. He had no idea of my bridge play but happened to pick a very good game to watch as subsequently, Val and I won.

Within half an hour of winning the competition, the charity sent out an email to all the entrants saying, "Thanks for supporting our event this afternoon and raising a lovely amount for charity. And, well done to Suzanne Anisfeld and Val for winning the competition."

That was very nice, I thought, and then I got changed and ready for my thirty-minute run. Before stepping out, I received a

Facebook notification on my mobile phone which I immediately looked at.

“Hi, Suzanne. This is Philip, Jeffrey’s brother. I don’t know if you remember me. Your name came up because you just won a bridge tournament that my brother was playing in.”

The two brothers, Philip and Jeffrey were old family friends that I hadn’t seen in over 35 years. If I hadn’t won, I would never have received this message because the charity didn’t provide a list of all the players, it only mentioned the winners. Backtracking, on the final round of the bridge event, we came across two players, whose names we didn’t know, as they had funny usernames which gave no clue as to who they might be. All we knew was that we were placed at Table 1 which meant that we were either in first or second position.

We asked our opponents their current percentage which happened to be higher than ours so realised that we were ranked second. After playing the round of two hands, we moved into first position as our opponents gave us top scores. Strangely enough, one of the opponents happened to be the mother of Jeffrey and Philip; so thanks Valerie for giving us two tops otherwise we would never have reconnected.

About a week later, I received a package in the post. “Congratulations on winning our first online charity bridge competition” on a compliment slip, together with a beautiful turquoise and white set of luxury playing cards. And my friend Val also received the same. As much as she appreciated the prize, she was desperate to win a trophy to put in pride of place on her mantelpiece.

Later that year, coming towards Christmas 2020, what a strange one it turned out to be. It was also my friend Val’s birthday, and I was wondering what to buy her for a present. Of course, it had to be a bridge trophy which I got engraved with a special birthday wish. I contacted her husband Mark and told him that I would drop the gift off to him on his doorstep but to keep it a secret from Val. I had sent a message to many of Val's friends to join a Zoom meeting the following evening where we could all wish her a Happy Birthday and present her with the trophy. She was absolutely delighted with her gift, although she was still desperate to be awarded another one for a competition win.

♣ ♦ ♠ ♥

No Trumps

20 January 2021, I had also arranged an online charity bridge tournament for CRUK to commence early afternoon, so we would be finished in time to watch the inauguration of President Joe Biden. Daniel had agreed to record a song with a friend, who lived abroad, on vocals. As I was getting to be quite an expert on Zoom, I invited all the bridge guests to join a meeting where I gave my welcome speech which stated,

"And by the way, your challenge today is to play every hand in 'No Trumps' and I certainly do not want any rioting at the bridge table." And then I shared screen with Daniel and Talia's song which of course was "Bridge Over Troubled Water".

By now, we were slowly getting back to some sort of normality. My Zoom bridge lessons stopped. Miss 120 and her group of friends decided to give bridge a miss and my other online group was now having face-to-face lessons with me, so I cancelled my Zoom account. A couple of months later, I received the following email:

> Sent: Thu, 22 Apr 2021 0:31
> Subject: Feedback about Zoom service
>
> Hi Suzanne,
>
> I am the CEO of Zoom. I am sorry to see that you recently cancelled your Zoom subscription. Our culture is to deliver happiness to our users, so I apologize that our service let you down…
>
> We value the input of each one of our customers and would greatly appreciate any feedback you can provide so that we can better meet your needs going forward.
>
> Thank you…

So here was my reply:

> Hi Eric,
>
> Thanks for your personal email message.
>
> Zoom has certainly not let me down and has been an absolute lifesaver during the pandemic. I was teaching bridge online which was the reason I had set up the account as the lessons were 2 hours long. Unfortunately, the lessons have now stopped so no longer need Zoom services for long periods of time. Perhaps you would like to learn bridge? Or you know people that wish to and then I can re-instate my account.
>
> Look forward to hearing from you.
>
> Kind regards

But I never got a response!

♣ ♦ ♠ ♥

Anyone Who Had a Heart

The summer came and we were now inviting friends for BBQs in the garden. On one occasion, I remember inviting Mandy and Steve for dinner and bridge. This would be our first face-to-face bridge game since March 2020 and we made sure that we had new packs of cards, new bidding boxes and of course, a hand sanitizer on the table. We had dinner outside first but had to move inside for the bridge as it was getting dark. The card table was all laid out ready and we had the patio doors wide open so we could get plenty of fresh air. Luckily, there was no wind so the cards wouldn't go flying.

"Don't be silly!" exclaimed Mandy, "we're not using cards!"

So, there we were sitting around the bridge table with our 4 iPads. My luxury cards will hopefully be used on a future occasion.

Irving and I were invited to Victor and Cassie's wedding in the summer of 2021. Victor is the brains behind the Café bridge events and is also the creator of the BRIAN bridge scoring system. We hadn't met Cassie before but were looking forward to meeting the new Mrs Bridge. The wedding was a few weeks after Freedom Day when the Government had just increased the numbers permitted for weddings and dancing was also allowed.

However, Victor and Cassie opted for a small wedding which was just beautiful, and we were most honoured to have been invited. We only recognized a couple of faces, but it seemed that most guests were bridge players. We were just a little disappointed that we didn't find any packs of cards on the tables! However, everything was perfect; the meal, the flowers, the string quartet, the speeches and even the weather couldn't have been any better.

I do remember the beginning of Victor's speech when he mentioned that he had Googled "Bride" for inspiration about his speech but unfortunately, Google kept on bringing up ideas to do with "Bridge"! Immediately after the speech, Victor and Cassie came over to our table to greet us, Victor still holding onto his speech. I could see that one of the pieces of paper was slightly folded and when I looked closer at the paper, I spotted some of the card symbols on the sheet.

"Victor, can I be nosey and have a quick look at your speech?"

He handed me his speech, and sure enough, on the reverse of all the pages were the layouts of the bridge hands from the club where he directed. I found this rather amusing to which Victor added,

"I didn't want to waste the paper."

Having reconnected with my friend Jeffrey, we arranged to get together, of course for a game of bridge. We obviously got chatting about the old days and reminisced about our youth. I also mentioned to him about cancelling my Café Bridge event due to the pandemic and he told me that he had previously attended a Café Bridge in Crouch End.

"When was that?" I asked. "I also played in a Café Bridge in Crouch End and had a fantastic meal in the best restaurant there."

It turned out that the date was the same and we were dining at the same restaurant. There was one long table of twenty; he was at one end and my partner and I were at the other. I wonder how many other times over the years our paths may have crossed!

Jeffrey told me about his grandfather who used to have regular bridge games with his friends for about forty years. The gentlemen were now all in their nineties. One sunny afternoon at the table, Fred asked to be excused while he was dummy. The hand was played and by the time it was finished, Fred had still not returned. The gentlemen waited for about ten minutes and thought they had better check up to see if Fred was ok.

Jeffrey's grandfather went to the bathroom to get Fred, but the bathroom was empty. He then happened to walk past the kitchen and could see that the back door was open. When he went to close it, he saw Fred through the glass pane, sitting down outside in the garden, so went to enquire what he was doing there.

"How lovely to see you, are you going to join me for a cup of tea?" asked Fred. He had completely forgotten that he was in the middle of a game of bridge.

Another member of my face-to-face teaching group, Rebecca, had a beautiful antique mahogany card table which she told me the story of. The table had belonged to her grandparents who were avid card players and it had been passed down to Rebecca's parents when they died. For many years, the card table sat in the garage collecting dust. Rebecca's parents were not card players but were hoping that one day, the table might be used by one of their children, so decided to keep it rather than put it up for auction. It most probably would have collected a pretty penny.

About fifteen years prior to my teaching Rebecca and her friends, she decided that she wanted to learn to play bridge and found three other friends, one of whom already played and was going to teach them all. She remembered that her parents had that beautiful table in their garage and asked them if she could borrow it. Of course, they were absolutely delighted to give it to her and knew that it was being put to good use.

Rebecca was very excited that she would be using her grandparents' card table. The other friends said that they would bring the other bridge equipment, bidding boxes, pens, bridge score sheets etcetera. Rebecca laid out a beautiful spread of homemade cakes, biscuits and fruit. The ladies arrived, sat down, and admired the most beautiful table. Josie took out the bridge cloth and covered the table, Joanna then placed the bridge score sheets and pens on the table followed by Rosalind's bidding boxes. And they were ready to go. But where were the playing cards? Of course, no one remembered to bring the cards and that was the end of them learning the game and the table resumed its home in the dusty garage.

One of my teaching groups all in fancy dress, of course, I am the Queen of Hearts!

My friend Sylvia decided to host a charity bridge event in her home, and we were all very excited about joining as this would be the first get-together in quite a while. I was to partner one of my friends, Michael, with whom I had been having regular online games during the lockdown; hoping that this time we would be using proper cards and not iPads. It was so good to be back playing face-to-face bridge again. Fortunately for us, we won so it really was a great afternoon. And even better for Michael as he was introduced to a lovely lady, and I believe that they are now dating and are regular bridge partners too.

♣ ♦ ♠ ♥

Winning Hand

Irving and I were booked in for a Café Bridge event taking place in Guildford in October 2021 and really looked forward to it. At one of Bernard's live seminars, he advertised the event and announced that he too would be playing in it. So having spent over one year watching him on seminars and YouTube bridge games, we were finally going to meet him.

The sun shone over Guildford and the hilly streets were filled with local shoppers, but you could recognize the Café Bridge entrants as they were walking around in pairs, holding their pieces of paper showing where they had to go. And what an afternoon it was, the people were lovely, the food was delicious, and the bridge was … well, we were very happy to beat Mr Magee and he ended up in second position.

Still running the CRUK bridge tournament and we decided to play our finals duplicate match online, using a new bridge platform Realbridge with the aid of camera and audio. In the past, online, you could literally be playing from your bed in your PJs but now felt obligated to get slightly dressed and made up.

Unfortunately, about a week before the match, both Irving and I developed the dreaded Coronavirus and were feeling pretty lousy. Irving decided he really wasn't up to playing but I really wanted to, especially as I was in charge. I was in contact with my first cousin who was a doctor and trying to arrange a home visit for me.

"I can get someone round on Monday night to see you?"

Of course, this was no good as I would be playing in the competition! Yes, bridge comes before health!

So, my friend Val agreed to partner me. I did feel slightly better by then but still didn't want people to see me online in my state, so switched my camera off. People couldn't believe that I was playing whilst suffering from Covid, but I did not let that affect my game and we ended up winning. Val was absolutely delighted with her bridge trophy which now takes pride of place on her mantelpiece.

Because of the huge amount of online bridge I was playing, I wanted to compare my results over the course of the year and see how well I was doing. I know I am Miss Spreadsheet, but I only know the very basic functions of Excel so had the wonderful assistance of Daniel. Here are the column entries on the spreadsheet:

Date	Competition	Partner	Percentage	Position	Number of pairs

And during the course of 2022, there were two hundred and ten entries and I have very pretty pictures of pie charts and graphs and some very interesting statistics.

I received an email from a charity organization advertising an event to be held in the summer. I saw the word "Bridge" in the title, together with a date which so happened to be my birthday. Most of the emails I receive go straight to the deleted folder, but I got excited about this one. And then I continued to open the email. To my disappointment, it was nothing about the card game but a London Bridges Walk which would take place early on a Sunday morning. Well, really It had my name written all over it as it was taking place on my birthday, and I am a keen walker, so I booked in to join with a friend. It was a delightful morning with plenty of sunshine and friendly faces, but I know where I would rather have been!

♣ ♦ ♠ ♥

Home Is Where The Heart Is

Going out for a beautiful summer afternoon walk down some of the local roads and avenues, I noticed that many of the houses were not numbered but had names. I was studying the names and wondered if these house names actually meant anything to their owners. Which got me thinking. I want one! But what could I call my house? Of course, it had to be something bridge-related. Trump House? Not sure that would go down too well with a certain US ex-president. The House of Spades? I didn't want to feel that my house had been turned into some sort of casino or bridge club. I've got it! And what is great is that I have managed to incorporate my children, Natalie and Daniel, into the name. So here goes, "Bridgend House" or should I say, "Bridge ND"? Well, that's my excuse anyway!

Mr Magee was very busy with his seminars and celebrating the two-year launch of his new website. He decided to offer some prizes, like some sort of raffle but you couldn't buy tickets. The way to enter his "raffle" was by leaving a review on social media or sending him a set hand on a given topic or basically anything to do with the game. So, I decided to write a poem:

There once was a man named Magee
Whose diet was just gluten-free
He taught so much bridge
Kept us away from the fridge
So, no cake or biscuits for tea.

His PowerPoints are a sensation
Providing great bridge to the nation
The love of the game
Has brought him to fame
How can you avoid such temptation?

Breaking transfers are one of his things
But you can see the confusion it brings
When bidding "no trumps"
Please don't get the grumps
With your partner who holds only kings.

Benji Acol, he loves this convention
But avoidance, I really must mention
His income assured
From cruises abroad
BMB will provide him a pension.

Wednesday nights with the teams are such fun
While Helen deals with Alfie, their son
One drink or two
Helps Bernard get through
And he's happy it's over and done.

I hope you've enjoyed my review
Free entry to the raffle I'm due
So, tune in online
And you'll be just fine
Cos Bernard will take care of you!

And what's more, I won a prize!

♣ ♦ ♠ ♥

High Low

I had a meeting organized in the afternoon in Stevenage which was expected to finish around half past four. That evening, we were going by tube to Charing Cross for a "Night of the Musicals". The plan was to drive straight to the tube station and meet Irving by approximately 6 o'clock to be in town with plenty of spare time. As I left the meeting just slightly after 4.30, the traffic was horrendous and I was worried I wouldn't make it.

It took about half an hour to get onto the A1 and by this stage, I was really panicking but fortunately, the road ahead looked pretty clear. I called Irving to tell him that I was running slightly late and just as I spoke, all the cars came to a complete halt. There had been a crash about thirty cars in front. The result of this was that I ended up getting stuck on the A1 for approximately three hours and unfortunately, missed the show.

However, back on the A1, everyone was getting out of their cars to see what was going on, police and ambulance were at the scene and it was **all hands on deck.** There was a queue of traffic going back for several miles. I got chatting with some of the people standing around me, one of whom was a DPD driver, worried about the lateness of all his deliveries. He then happened to ask me and some of the others standing with me,

"I don't suppose anyone has a pack of cards on them?"

Well, he had certainly come to the right person, and I went straight to the boot of my car where I had a selection of bridge equipment which I use for my teaching. I handed him a bridge wallet that contained a pack of cards; the wallet consisted of four pouches which held thirteen cards in each section, so he knew I was a bridge player.

"You play bridge?" he inquired. "Fancy a game?"

We both logged onto BBO and played. Who needs musical theatre when you can get your very own game of bridge on the motorway?

What else are motorways for?

We heard that there was another Café Bridge event taking place in Guildford so, of course, we had to book in to defend our title. Irving came to pick me up and what should have been a ten-minute journey to my house took him forty-five minutes. He was in a foul mood. He was worried that we wouldn't get to Guildford in time for 11 o'clock and wondered what was the point of even going. I convinced him that the journey to my house was through the rush hour and the M25 should now be clear so let's go. And we did, and we made it.

It was a glorious sunny day, of course, the sun always shines on Café Bridge. However, the bridge was lousy. We could not do anything right. Unfortunately, we couldn't blame it on the cards as everyone had the same ones. It just wasn't our day. Using Victor's brilliant BRIAN bridge-scoring mobile app, we could see how badly we were doing, and it was pretty grim.

As we were getting into the final round of the competition, we arrived at the pub and took our seats whilst waiting for our opponents to join us. We had time to check who we would be playing and worked out that they were in fifth position. I will call these gentlemen John and Mike for the purpose of this book. I think we were about sixtieth out of over eighty pairs, so we had a bit of work to do! They were two board rounds and the first board we played against them gave them a good score, so it was all on the last board. John on my right, opened the bidding with "one diamond" and then there were three consecutive passes, so he had won the auction.

I contemplated my lead which was a difficult one as I had all four Queens but opted for the Queen of Clubs as I had a doubleton. Mike laid his cards on the table as he was the "dummy". During some time in the play, another club was played, and Irving realized that I now had no more clubs in my hand. We were playing the hand at a steady pace and could see that they were struggling to make their contract. It was now Irving to play a card as he had won the previous trick. He knew that both John and I had no more clubs so he opted to play a winning club as I could overruff (trump higher) John's card, should John decide to trump.

John thought and he thought, and he hesitated, and he thought and about three minutes into his thought process, I picked up the other traveller on a table on my right and then turned back to the left to ask Mike if he would put it in the large bag behind him.

Then I turned back where I could see the King of Diamonds on the table, so I followed suit and put down my Five of Diamonds.

As soon as I put my card on the table, I realised that it wasn't John on lead but Irving's Nine of Clubs so there was no need for me to play a diamond. Why would I play a little diamond underneath the King? So, I quickly picked up my card and then placed the Three of Spades on the table.

"You cannot do that!" John shrieked.

"Yes, she can!" Irving exclaimed. "Can't you see that it was an honest mistake? Why would she want to under trump your King? My girlfriend was only trying to help. It's the last hand of the day and she just wanted to help clear up and tidy away the hands."

Irving was not happy. He wasn't happy before this but now he was really unhappy. I didn't really care; the bridge was so lousy, and I just wanted to go home.

"Let's call the director," insisted John, which we did, and he came straight over to sort out the argument.

"I want you to continue playing the hand and I will look into the scoring at the end of the tournament and will do what is fair."

Well, he couldn't be fairer than that, but Irving got up out of his chair, threw his remaining cards on the table and started shouting expletives at John, which I am not going to repeat. And then he stormed off effing and blinding under his breath. I was so embarrassed and wondered how I was going to get home from Guildford, assuming he was going to drive off without me.

"I am so sorry for my partner's outburst, there is no justification for what he just said but I do understand why he said it and I think it is rather unfair. This is just a friendly charity game and not a serious competition."

At which point, I picked up my bag and jacket and headed towards the car park where fortunately I found Irving.

Back at the bridge club during the week when it was relatively quiet, we arrived slightly late so didn't get our first choice of seats, the East/West position. So, I sat in North as I liked to take control of the Bridgemate. We had just finished our first round, and the percentages were shown as 50% - 50%. When you click on the OK button, it then gives you the names of your next opponents. Oh, my goodness, there was a very unusual surname that I had recognized. And as the two gentlemen took their seats, I asked if they happened to know this person whom I hadn't seen in twenty-four years.

"He happens to be my father."

To which I responded in amazement, so all the others could hear me, "He happened to be my gynaecologist."

Which brought back fond memories of my pregnancy days and playing bridge in that hospital bed.

♣ ♦ ♠ ♥

Novices

I am currently teaching bridge to a group of Year 5 primary school children as well as supervising bridge at a residential daycare centre for the elderly. The kids are great and literally like sponges. On one occasion, I told the children that they really had to try to play a bit quicker to prepare themselves for an Interschools competition taking place the following month. One little boy piped up,

"But Suzanne, you told us that bridge is a slow game!"

I also told another group of Year 5 children how fascinating the game is and even I am still constantly learning, to which another boy said,

"Why are you teaching us if you are still learning?"

Straight after teaching the kids, I drive to the leisure centre and meet up with some friends for a game of badminton. They are not bridge players, but they always question me on how my week has been and what I have been up to, even though they know that bridge will definitely get a mention. As I am still in bridge mode pretty much all day long, I don't focus very well on the badminton. When certain scores on the badminton court arise, I will state:

1-2 – one two, that'll do (the only bridge-related statement)

2-2 – Desmond

6-15 – is that the time already?

7-11 – open twenty-four hours

9-11 – I don't like that date

18-12 – the 1812 Overture (to which I start humming)

20-12 – London Olympics

And I think my friends have just got used to my crazy scoring comments but to top it all, when I am holding the shuttlecock in the middle of the game, I announce, "Whose deal is it?!"

I am not sure which one will come first but my hope is that one day, either I will win at badminton 21-0 or be dealt thirteen of one suit from a shuffled pack of cards. And when that day arrives, I am going to treat myself to a very large and expensive present.

♣ ♦ ♠ ♥

Hearts and Diamonds

A few months ago, we were playing in a league match at someone's home. During the evening, my phone started ringing but I decided not to answer as I didn't want to disturb the game. I looked at the phone and noticed it was a Facetime call from Natalie who was in South America. I told the others that it was a shame I had missed the call as she was probably standing by "Christ the Redeemer" on Sugarloaf Mountain and wanted to show me the sights. I switched the phone to silent and put it back into my handbag.

About an hour later, we stopped for coffee and I took my phone out. I could see about six missed calls from Natalie and a WhatsApp message asking me to call her as soon as possible. Panic going through my mind, I called her back immediately.

"Mum, I've been trying to get hold of you for the last hour and now you are literally the last to know, Nick's just proposed, we're engaged!"

But of course, didn't I tell you earlier? Bridge always comes first!

Organising the league for the CRUK involves quite a lot of hard work. Apart from arranging the venue for the finals, the raffle prizes and booking the tournament director, I have the job of putting people into leagues. The competition is a London-based one and I have to be aware of all the postcodes. I try my best to put people into their local area but also have requests from players that they do not wish to play against certain individuals. And there is also the fact that I have a couple of players who were previously married but now playing with their new spouses. Not to mention that I heard through the grapevine that a gentleman who was partnering his wife was having an affair with one of the other players. It's such an arduous task, rather like a seating plan for a wedding. Natalie and Nick, I wish you all the best!

No game is complete without a few hearts and diamonds.

♣ ♦ ♠ ♥

End Play

Recently, Irving and I were playing a duplicate game on Realbridge and after the first round, we were in the bottom position below 20%. Our opponents were at the top. We had a bit of a joke with the gentleman and Irving said,

"Oh well, the only way is up and for you, the only way is down!"

I added, "Maybe we will meet you in the middle?"

Well, for the whole evening, these men remained in the top position, but we could see ourselves slowly climbing up. In the penultimate round, we moved into third position and it all got very exciting. In the last round, our friendly opponents gave up three top scores and we saw our names move into second position. Eighteen boards had been played by most of the players, however, the pair in top position were still showing as seventeen boards being played. I went to get a cup of coffee whilst waiting for them to complete the last hand and Irving then gave a big scream,

"We've won! We've won!"

The moral of the story is, even when you are at your lowest, never give up!

One of my regrets is not having taught bridge to my parents. They did start having lessons about twenty years ago but were keen travellers at that time and didn't stay around long enough in the UK for their lessons. I know they would have loved it, already regularly playing Kalooki and Scrabble. Another thing that upsets me is that my children have no interest in it. They think that they are far too young to play but I was even younger than them when I started. They too, would be great players as they are both mathematical and enjoy other card games. When I go to bridge clubs and see a parent and child partnership, there is a little envy in me as this is one of my dreams. Hopefully, by the time they have read my book, they may soon change their minds and ask me to teach them.

However, recently I played in a league Teams match against a local boys' school and I'm pleased to say that they absolutely thrashed us. I was so delighted to be beaten by a group of teenage boys and very happy to know that the future of this wonderful game is in very safe hands.

Getting everything organised for the CRUK 44th bridge duplicate finals at the Acol Bridge Club, I had a few raffle prizes that had been donated but I also needed to get something for the winners. I always like to give trophies as prizes as I believe it is a nice memento of the occasion. Some people would rather win a box of chocolates or a voucher, but this is something that will be gone in five minutes whilst the trophy is an everlasting memory of a great win.

I picked up the trophies from the shop and showed them to Irving who asked if I had bought any for the runners-up. In previous years, I had purchased them for the runners-up but decided this year only to provide them for the winners as our takings were down because we didn't have as many applicants. So, I didn't want to spend the charity's money. However, Irving decided that we really should provide the runners-up with some sort of prize, so I ordered a couple more smaller trophies. And I am so pleased that I listened to him as you will never guess who came second in the competition!

I was standing in the grounds of a local cemetery listening to a eulogy given about a wonderful lady who was the dear mother of a friend of mine. I was talking to my friend Val who pondered,

"I wonder what people will say about me when I am no longer here. They will probably mention the fact that I am a maths teacher and throw a calculator into the grave. And as for you, Suzanne, of course, everyone will talk about your obsession with bridge and throw in a couple of packs of cards!"

And this gave me the idea that when I do die, I need three other bridge players buried near me, but we must be in the correct North South/East West positions.

I've heard there's a bridge club in the dead centre of town!

And to you, my friend Val, I bequeath all my bridge trophies to be displayed on your mantelpiece, hoping this will bring back very fond memories of all our games together.

Apart from my new house name, my home has many objets d'art which of course are bridge-related. Little pictures of all the card symbols greet you as you enter the hallway, drinks coasters, dishes, mugs, oven gloves, I have even had a mural painted on my wall which is basically a tree filled with the card symbols, musical notes, fruit and initials which make up my family tree. I do believe that I am slightly addicted, and my children think I am crazy, but I guess, there are worse addictions one could have.

On looking at my mobile telephone, you can see that I have so many different WhatsApp groups, some of which I will list below:

Big Bridge, County Bridge Challenge, Sunday afternoon Bridge, Sunday Bridge, Wednesday bridge group, Friday bridge group, Online bridge partners, Suzy bridge lessons, Walker's bridge group, Teams bridge BBO, Bridge, Thursday bridge, Beginners bridge, Heath Bridge, Bridge 4 Us, Inspirational Bridge, Bridge lesson, Bridge ladies. I think that's enough, don't you?

As a secondary school child, I used to love my maths lessons and we had the best teacher ever. However, English Language was another story! Embarrassingly, it took me several attempts to pass my O-Level. Having left college to start work, I was so relieved that never in my life would I have to do another comprehension or write another essay. But now, I find that I have just completed writing this book! I am rather proud of myself and hope that you have enjoyed the stories. If you have, I would be delighted to hear from you. Alternatively, if you would like to set up a new Bridge WhatsApp group, that's fine too, or if you just want to have a game, then give me a call.

♣ ♦ ♠ ♥

Glossary of Bridge Terms used in this book

Auction: a series of bids or calls which are made by the four players in clockwise fashion to determine the final contract.

Bid: a number (1 through 7) followed by the name of a suit or no trump (1♥, 3NT, 7♦, etc.).

Bidding box: a box placed on the table that contains cards with bids on them. By selecting and playing a card from the box, a player can make a bid without speaking. Bidding boxes are mainly used in bridge clubs where duplicate bridge is played.

Blackwood: a 4NT bid used to ask your partner to show how many Aces they hold when looking to bid a slam and 5NT asks how many Kings your partner holds when looking to bid a grand slam.

Call: any bid, pass, double or redouble.

Contract: the final suit and level of bidding sets the number of tricks and the trump suit for the game.

Declarer: the player who made the first bid during the auction of the suit of the final contract.

Defenders: The pair that tries to defeat the contract.

Dummy: the declarer's partner is the dummy and after the opening lead has been made by the opposition, the dummy lays all their cards on the table face up. The dummy has no more play in the game for that particular hand and normally makes a cup of tea!

Duplicate: a form of bridge where every deal is played at several tables and scores on each deal are subsequently compared.

Face card: King, Queen, or Jack.

Fit: a combined partnership holding at least 8 cards in a suit.

Grand slam: a contract to win all 13 tricks.

Major suit: hearts ♥ and spades ♠

Minor suit: clubs ♣ and diamonds ♦

No trumps (NT): a contract or a bid without a trump suit.

Opponent: a member of the other partnership or team.

Pass: a bid that shows that the player does not wish to change the contract named by the preceding bid.

Stayman: An artificial response of 2♣ to an opening bid of 1NT asking if partner holds a 4-card major suit.

Suit: clubs ♣, diamonds ♦, hearts ♥, and spades ♠.

Teams: a form of duplicate bridge which is played with 8 players at 2 tables. The North-South pair at one table are teammates with the East-West pair at the other table.

Trick: a set of 4 cards where each person plays 1 card in turn. There are 13 tricks in a game of bridge.

Trump: a suit of cards with the highest ranking over the other suits in a particular hand.

Printed in Great Britain
by Amazon

42212280R00046